THE MIRROR OF LIGHT

THE
MIRROR
OF LIGHT

RODNEY COLLIN

SHAMBHALA
Boston & London
1985

SHAMBHALA PUBLICATIONS, INC.
314 Dartmouth Street
Boston, Massachusetts 02116

SHAMBHALA PUBLICATIONS, INC.
at Routledge & Kegan Paul
14 Leicester Square
London WC2H 7PH

First Shambhala edition
Printed in the United States of America
Distributed in the United States by Random House
and in Canada by Random House of Canada Ltd.

Library of Congress Cataloging in Publication Data
Collin, Rodney.
The mirror of light.
Reprint. Originally published: London : Watkins, 1959.
1. Spiritual life—Miscellanea.   I. Title.
BF1999.C6778   1984   299   84-22141
ISBN 0-87773-314-7 (pbk.)
ISBN 0-394-72996-X (Random House)

EDITOR'S FOREWORD

Most of the notes of which this book is composed were found among Rodney Collin's papers after his death. Some had already been used as a basis for talks to his associates, others had been put by for future use. It is impossible to say which he wrote himself and which come from other sources. He had collected them as material for those who have passed beyond the preliminary stage of self-study. To these notes have been added others, taken of his conversations with his friends.

The expression 'self-remembering' is a special term used by G. I. Gurdjieff, P. D. Ouspensky, Maurice Nicoll and others of the same tradition. Its meaning is explained in the context.

The 'Fourth Way' is the balanced combination of the three traditional ways of re-union with God – those of physical, mental and emotional control. It is the development of the whole man, situated in the ordinary circumstances of daily life and dedicated to the realization of his highest possibilities.

Acknowledgement is made to Mema Dickins and all others who have helped with the collection and arrangement of these notes.

JANET COLLIN SMITH
Mexico, October 1958

INTRODUCTION

We live our life in a mirror; everything is reversed. When we see a scene it is received in the brain reversed. The rays go out, cross and are received in reverse. Reality exists in the place where the two lines cross, if we can find it.

The same takes place in our thoughts; we think that cause is effect and effect, cause. For us, the physical is more real than the spiritual. That which our senses perceive we call objective, while all that is imperceptible to our physical senses we call unreal or imaginary. We think sowing and reaping are essentially different and fail to understand that they are the same. We regard birth and death as antitheses and have altogether forgotten that to die is to be born.

The life we live, the world we live in, is a mirage. If we understand a mirage we understand a miracle.

We should study more about the mirror. It is the key of the book that should soon be written.

RODNEY COLLIN, *1955*

7

I

Every living body emits irradiations. They are electrical. Whenever anything is touched it collects irradiations. We would understand this better if we remembered the idea of the mirror. Everything reflects back. Places where people have had strong emotions are full of strong irradiations, either negative or positive. Inanimate objects reflect the irradiations of living creatures.

There is an exception to this. In ultra-heavy matter energy has become condensed to such a point that it escapes. Ultra-heavy matter is dangerous because instead of reflecting irradiations, it emits them. The earth needs a minimum of emissory material, but men are accumulating too much of it. This is why this is a kairos time, a time of exceptional opportunity for those who want to acquire will, love and reason. A great change is approaching in which positive forces must balance negative ones. The positive irradiations emitted by people of good will collect the neutral irradiations emitted by ultra-heavy matter and form them into a protective barrier like a kind of jelly that absorbs and neutralizes negative irradiations. We project all the time, either negativeness or positiveness. To positive irradiations are added neutral irradiations, in proportion to the strength of the positive ones.

It does not matter what we think about other people, but it does matter what we project. To think good or bad about them affects nobody – it neither helps nor hurts. But we do not realize how much our projections affect other people. If one says: 'So and so is ridiculous', that will not hurt him. But if one says: 'I love you' with a negative feeling, that will do harm. We do not realize the responsibility we have for everything we project. We have to project positiveness. Negativeness flows out of us and reflects on other people. It affects thousands of people all over the world. If we have positive irradiations they help not only us but other people, also all over the world. We must be very careful to project sincerity and strength. If we project positive irradiations we can leave their distribution to God. Those who have seen truth irradiate goodness; we cannot imagine how strong these irradiations are nor to what tremendous distances they can reach.

We are like radios. The moment we are negative we may tune in to the accumulated negativeness of someone, perhaps thousands of miles distant, who has been negative for years. There are many, many different wave-lengths, but there is always someone who has the same wave-length as our own, whom we affect and who affects us if we let him. That is one reason why it is so necessary to guard against being negative, in order not to collect the negativeness of other people and add it to our own. And think of the responsibility if we send negativeness to someone else. It might be someone who is just getting out of a negative state and whom we push back again by our negativeness. Some people are built so that they collect negativeness and others positiveness, so we cannot judge them. We must just be careful not to send out negativeness, but positiveness instead.

When we are in harmony with each other we produce a very high energy that goes hundreds of miles to people who need it. If we have no harmony inside us we cannot project it. Positive irradiations are made by will. When we have found our real selves we will be able to irradiate positiveness.

We can find proof of the strength of our irradiations in the way they can change the weather. Sometimes in a drouth people carry the image of a saint in procession and pray to it for rain. When the rain comes they think the saint has worked a miracle. In reality the force of their concentrated irradiations changed the atmospheric pressure and enabled moisture to be precipitated. People with faith knew this long ago by experience and science is beginning to find it out.

One unit of positiveness reflects one hundredfold, but one unit of negativeness reflects a thousandfold. When reflected, each is magnified. That is why, when we turn negativeness into positiveness, the result is two thousandfold. Negativeness is much stronger. Bless negativeness that makes positiveness. It all depends on the level of the person how negative thoughts are used. A person of low level uses them negatively, in a very low form; one of a higher level can turn them into positiveness. If we are absolutely positive ourselves we can turn negative irradiations into tremendous force. We have to collect them first by attention. To turn negative irradiations positive we must be completely positive ourselves. If we doubt, even for a second, nothing can be done because we are already negative. If we see something unpleasant or gruesome we must find something funny in it and laugh, and point it out to other people if they are being affected by the unpleasantness. If we see someone reacting negatively we must try to make ourselves positive by laughing or not believing it. That is why it is possible to collect energy at a movie when the audience is horrified at a murder film. We have to be strong enough not to let the negativeness make us negative too. But then we become much stronger by turning it. Once we start turning it we can keep it turning; it keeps turning almost by itself. If we can be positive for an hour and then another hour and then another hour we purify our instincts and reactions. When we catch a bad thought in ourselves we can check it, change it and make it into a much stronger good thought. If we are completely positive we can counteract someone else's bad thought, no matter how bad it is, and turn it to good.

We are connected with everyone we have met or talked to or felt, because we have given them part of ourselves – our irradiations. It is not performance but irradiations that matter. Our reactions are physical; we have to make them positive. If we think of ourselves everything goes wrong. If we forget ourselves we can do right. We cannot love everybody, but we are here to project harmony. If we have harmony we grow. To collect positiveness we must love people, really love them. Just love them. Everyone is in need of love; it is spiritual food. When we love people we give them our flesh and blood. Blood is emanations, flesh means our real self. To love is not an emotion nor a sensation nor an idea; it is the particular kind of irradiation that only a certain type of action can produce in us. If a person feels affection for someone but is too lazy to help him, he does not love him. On the other hand a person may feel very irritated with someone, but if in spite of his impatience he makes an effort to help him, that is loving him. He projects to him irradiations that probably are of more help than his action, but which can only be set in motion by action with the intention to help. The only way to love our neighbour as ourself is to learn how to communicate with God. Then we have the grace to love both our neighbour and ourself.

All functions are biological. Just as the body functions are biological, so emotions have a biological basis. There are two kinds of negativeness. The kind that comes from inside is meanness; this is bad. But the negativeness that comes from outside is reaction; this is not bad. Often when we react irritably it is because we have an accumulation of body acids that need to be eliminated. We need to have an elimination of these acids at least once a week, in anger or tears or strong laughter. The mistake is when we identify ourselves with these eliminations and mix them with feelings. It is wrong to stop anyone from this kind of elimination; it does them harm in the same way it would do harm to stop a physical elimination. Babies are very wise; they know about this. They will cry till they are red in the face. Mothers should not pick them up till they have finished, though they must not be left to cry too long or they will form the habit. We must learn how to get rid of our emotional waste. Once a week we should run, shout, laugh, cry, put it out of us. We should get rid of our physical reactions, but not against other people. We must know the difference between physical reactions, and feelings. We must never hurt anybody; apart from that it does not matter how we work off our emotional waste. When we have eliminated it we will be clean.

The cleaner we are outside the cleaner inside. If we are clean the pores of the skin are ready to get rid of acids and we will be more healthy. Cleanliness depends on how we were brought up. We have to be clean as a base, to be virile, strong. Our houses should be clean. There is a Russian saying: 'Where there is dust there is a devil'. God only comes into clean things. When we understand cleanliness we have to cultivate neatness. We should always be aware of neatness, for it helps very much with self-respect. After neatness comes smartness, a combination of quality, suitability and fashion that is within the reach of everyone with taste and intelligence. It does not of necessity mean being dressed in the latest fashion, for often fashion means making oneself look ridiculous in order not to be thought ridiculous.

When instead of saying: 'I feel so lazy today', we turn our lethargy into positiveness by saying: 'I must do something to get out of this', we find that we have more energy than if we gave in to it. We must try to convert our negativeness into positiveness. We must make everything positive by our wish, by our strength, by our efforts. If there is one person who is depressed in a gathering of people he can make everyone else depressed too. But if we come in and say to ourselves: 'This cannot go on. I am strong; I can change it by being positive', the atmosphere in the room will change. We must not allow negativeness. The stronger person wins. If the stronger person projects negativeness, negativeness wins. Whatever is strongest affects whatever is weakest. A crowd can be on the verge of panic and one strong person, by projecting confidence, can stop it. In a group of people who are trying to work one person can raise the whole level. We can never make the excuse that there are some in the group that keep the whole on a low level, because *one* person can change the rest – just one person. Supposing you come into a room and find four people quarrelling. You go to one of them and say 'hello'. You can say it in such a way that it changes his mood. Then you go to the next one, or even smile at him. If you are sufficiently strong and positive yourself you will change him, and so on with all four. People *cannot* be negative in the presence of someone who is really positive.

Negativeness comes when we feel or see something ugly or dirty or mean and let it come into us. We should recognize and measure negativeness but not let it come into us. If we prevent negativeness from coming inside it becomes less and less.

We should never be depressed about things we have done that seem to us now were bad. Nothing is bad in itself. Life is a ladder; we must put our feet on each rung and step up from it. Bad is down a rung, good is up. But no rung is bad or good in itself. There is nothing good or bad; there is positive and negative, whichever we make ourselves. We must not think so much of ourselves and of the past. Feel how exciting is the coming. That really is exciting.

Energy is like small cells in the air which attract others of the same kind. There are two kinds of energy – negative and positive. We know what is negative and what is positive. We must face what we are thinking. If it is negative we must say to ourselves: 'This is a negative thought. It may be pleasant, but I don't want it.' Then if we think about something else, or read a book, the thought will go. Up to the tenth time it will be hard, but the eleventh time it will be easy. We must make good habits. It is just as easy to make good habits as bad ones. We cannot know what is good or bad, but we can recognize right actions and wrong actions.

People often blame their state of mind on external influences. There are no external influences, only internal ones. If someone is negative towards us it cannot affect us as long as it remains outside. It can only affect us if we let it come inside, bring it inside us. How else can someone else's negativeness affect us? It can only affect us if we allow it inside us by making it our own. Then what was external becomes internal because we ourselves make it so by giving it our attention.

If we relax we will never get tired, but if we try to control our attention we get tired very soon. If we do not try to force our attention it will not wander; we will collect our energy instead of losing it. Relax and everything will come. We relax when we forget ourselves. We can rest by smiling; immediately the whole

16

body relaxes and rests. We must learn to relax our muscles, especially at the back of the shoulders. We should try to feel our spine from the skull down to the bottom – feel it and have control over it. Then we will not be tired. We know that our body has a limitation and will get tired if it goes beyond that limitation. We know that if we do not sit straight we will get tired. If we do not sit straight it is our fault if we get tired. Either our body commands us or we command our body. By will power we can train our body to do more. We have to go little by little.

It makes us tired to draw in again the air we breathe out. When we are tired and depressed it is because we are getting back the same energy we are expelling. The remedy for this kind of tiredness is to move – move mentally, that is, direct our attention away from ourselves and make it follow a definite line, and if possible move physically with a purpose.

We must collect our feelings. When we try to collect ourselves, our aura grows stronger. When it does that, the negative feelings of other people cannot reach us. They can only penetrate the outer fringe of our aura. If we collect ourselves frequently and strongly we cannot be touched. It is said that by concentrating himself Cagliostro could throw somebody down a yard away by the force of his aura. There are strange stories in the Acts; when somebody did something against the Apostles they would suddenly be struck dead. Perhaps their own negativeness was thrown back at them. Every energy we project comes back. When we are tired we cannot project clearly.

The most powerful projection and terrible force in the world is fear. It compels men to seek happiness, develop civilizations and start wars. Fear is behind all the irrationality and chaotic emotions that dog mankind. The old prophets knew the power of fear; all the holy books recognize it. We must understand what it means to leave fear behind. To understand the big work we must not have any kind of fear. It is the mother of hatred.

Little hates grow into big hates. We cannot allow them any more. We may call them misunderstandings or by any other name we like. Out of them come wars and all awful things. We must get rid of them. Then will come harmony.

Even if a person is negative now, probably one day he will grow out of it and understand. It does not matter what we see in other people, what horrible things we see in them. There is only one way to help people who hate: to show them real love and humility. But by actions, not by words. Probably there will be a strong reaction, but in the end it will work. There is a heart in everybody; if that is touched, they understand. When they see someone sincere they hear what he says. If we project sincerity, truthfulness and honesty, they will feel it. They may not recognize it at the moment, but one day they will. If we are honest, truthful and sincere with ourselves we will be the same with other people and something of that they will feel. Some day they will recognize it. We must reach people more by feelings than by words. There is a good side to everyone; there is no one who is completely bad, as there is no one who is completely good. No one is perfect or he would not be here.

People do not understand the tremendous force of negativeness because they do not want to be responsible for it. We must not feed any negative emotions. If we take our difficulties seriously we feed them. If we say to something we do not want, such as vanity: 'Excuse me!' it will leave us. We must try to float over the top of difficulties, not wallow in them. It is very important to stay above all annoyances. If we feel light and happy we will be ourselves.

What is it to be oneself? It means to be one's positive self. People say: 'I was born with a bad temper; that is how I am.' That is exactly *not* being oneself. To *be* means to be positive. To be negative means not to be. Negativeness, zero, a minus quantity by definition *is not*. A positive force by its very nature gives out. To be ourselves we must give – give attention, give interest, give whatever we can at every moment. Then we are ourselves, we have being.

First comes respect, then love, then harmony. First we must respect ourselves. Charity begins at home; that means in ourselves. Someone who says: 'I am stupid, I am vulgar, I am bad' is blaspheming God, because God is in everyone. It is true that we are all temples of the Holy Ghost. When we realize that we have done something stupid or vulgar or wrong we should say: 'This is in me; I will take it out of me because it does not belong in me; for my own self-respect, because my real self is not like this, I will not act like this.' When we act wrongly we are *acting*, behaving in a way that is not in accordance with what we are. We cannot *act* rightly; we can only *be* right, and then our behaviour is in accordance with what we are. We should not try to *do* things – just *be*. Be ourselves, love God, be friends with our neighbour. Friendship means being alert to the needs of one's neighbour and ready to help him. To say: 'What can I do for my neighbour?' is to think of oneself. To *be*, alert, open, loving, is all that is necessary. Then one will act rightly without trying to do right. To be oneself is to obey one's conscience. Conscience is our alarm-clock.

Everyone has three kinds of time – his own, that of nature and that of the sun. We have to check our clocks by the time of the sun. Conscience means relating our time to the other two times – of nature, that is, of the world in which we live, our neighbours; of the sun, that is, God.

Time exists only on this physical level. When we have reached *being* there is neither past nor future; there is only being. When we *are*, we *are* every minute. Then we have found liberty, happiness, beauty. And beauty is love.

Where there is love, God is within us. Wherever we see something beautiful, God is there. God made all that is beautiful; it is man who makes ugliness. Real love does not stop at a person or an object; if it is real it goes on to God. Nothing real ever disappears. If it disappears it is not real. What is not true always disappears for it has never been.

We must forget ourselves. When we find something beautiful we should lose ourselves in it; this is ecstasy.

Ecstasy is the contemplation of reality. It is real emotion. Ecstasy is the opposite of imagination. If we see something beautiful we are experiencing something real. We are seeing a fact. If we take things into ourselves we make them small, lose them. If we lose ourselves in things bigger than ourselves, we lose our small selves and find our real selves.

To be ourselves we must have courage of will. We are so full of our own acting we do not notice it ourselves and forget that everyone else can see that we are putting on an act. The only ones we deceive are ourselves. If we do not act we can be ourselves. That is more comfortable, because we do not have to remember what role we played before.

We should come back to ourselves every day, be ourselves without imitation. Everyone should find in himself what he can do, even if it is done badly at first. Everybody must work and make the best of his work. Everybody must *be* something through his work. First point: to aim to know oneself; second point: to know that one does not know oneself; third point: to know oneself, to be oneself. To find something that does not change, that is to find oneself. How to find it? By what we see in other people. That which shocks us in other people is what we have in ourselves; that which we respect in other people we have in ourselves too. If we recognize a quality in someone else, that means we have it ourselves.

If we have a fault, we know someone else has it too. If we feel that someone is negative it means that we are feeding our own negativeness. When we label something we are not labelling it but ourselves. If we speak negatively about a person we are really talking about ourselves. We paint ourselves with the colours we paint other people. When people say something nasty about us, it is never really about us; it is themselves they are talking about, because they only see in others the reflection of themselves. So if people say unpleasant things about us we can only be sorry for them, sorry that they are so small, even if our conscience tells us that we caused their talk by something we did. We identify with what they say because our conscience tells us we caused it. That is why fear of people is imagination.

One reason why it is so important to find our real selves is that no one can hurt us. No one knows who we are. Others can see the outside but not the inside, the real self. We must be individual, to make our souls strong. Your soul can make mine stronger, mine can make yours stronger. Twenty strong people could change the world – pure, good, strong individuals. There could be peace, always peace and harmony if there were only twenty men who understood and practised harmony.

Everything is so simple, within our reach. We are the ones who complicate it. Why is it we do not understand that being ourselves, being real, is everything? But even those words we do not understand. To be ourselves, this is the work. Work begins when we learn to separate ourselves from what we are not, when we get the taste of our true selves. Why do we do that? Not to please ourselves, but to have something real and clean to offer to God. Christ said: 'Leave all you have and follow Me.' That did not mean that we should leave all the circumstances of our lives. It meant leave the falseness in ourselves and be our real selves. Only the real self can follow Him.

II

Marriage is a cross, and a very heavy one. It is by no means all sweetness and there is much work to be done. Both partners have to break their habits; their work is to adapt themselves to each other. True marriage is a state of perfect polarity of the individuals, for the woman, if she works on herself, becomes more a woman, and the man, if he works too, becomes more a man. Anyone who has been married knows how difficult it is to make a marriage harmonious and produce the true spiritual union that lasts for ever. Physical union loses its attraction in three or four months when it has become a habit, but on the level of the spirit ever new bonds of union are created, which become a source of constantly renewed happiness.

When she marries, a wife has the duty and obligation to make her husband completely happy, and the husband has the duty and obligation to make his wife completely happy. Both are responsible for the happiness of the other.

The home should be pure and holy. How is this accomplished? The work of making a home harmonious and happy is not for or by the husband or wife; it is the work of God. Because of this, those who marry take great responsibilities, but receive blessing and grace – that is, if they do the work of God, a work that is truly holy. Married couples have the obligation of teaching their children how to project harmony, but by deeds and not by words.

When a woman marries she ceases to be Miss So-and-So and becomes Mrs X. She has to forget herself in order to live for her husband. Here true work begins – *to forget oneself.* The wife should never separate herself from her husband. She must guess his thoughts and fulfil his wishes even if she is worn out with fatigue and to do so means more work and further efforts for her. And the more a husband is a real man the more he will cherish his wife, respect her and protect her.

How many young people in love want to get married, but she has family problems and he, economic ones? They take these questions seriously and quite rightly so, but which is more important, to work for a salary or for that which brings no money but is the work of God? When there is real love there are no problems; they are only created by vanity and selfishness.

When two people marry they make a promise to God. If they divorce they not only break that promise made to God and to each other but they break something that has grown between them. A woman who gives herself to a man gives him something more than her body; she gives him part of herself for always. What she gives her husband and he to her binds them into one.

Our irradiations are 'coloured' by the chemics of the body. Each person has different chemics. This accounts for the attraction, repulsion or indifference between people. We should remember that, to people whose chemics we do not like, ours are equally repellent. We must go beyond them, then the difficulty will not come back. People are attracted to each other if their chemics are different and complementary. Particles of their chemics interchange until they have become balanced. Then the attraction ceases and the two people are indifferent to each other. This is why marriages based on physical attraction always come to grief.

If a marriage is the result of only physical attraction the sexual feelings that marriage arouses are attached by association to chemical reactions. When the husband and wife no longer exchange chemical particles through irradiation they become attracted to other people and their sexual feelings follow. If, however, people marry because they have attraction for each other on a higher level, really love each other, their sexual feelings become attached to real love and not to chemical reactions. They increase and become more natural and the two people help each other to grow. When sexual feelings are aroused before or outside of marriage they must be controlled. And sexual feelings should never be controlled because it is dangerous to do so. All kinds of physical and emotional disturbances result. Sexual feelings do not depend on chemics. The fact that the man is a man and the woman is a woman is enough to arouse them. Naturally this does not mean that people should marry although their chemics repel each other. They should obey their instinct about this, while remembering that imagination can easily make them believe that physical attraction is mental and spiritual affinity, whereas it has no connection with them whatsoever.

It is very important that young people should be taught about irradiations. If they understood the real facts of marriage they would not later have to control their sexual feelings in relation to others who are not their marriage partners. Husbands and wives who have sexual relations with others than their marriage partners do themselves great harm. They divide the flow of their finest irradiations and receive mixed irradiations in return, with the result that their soul is weakened. At death their spirit will have an inadequate vehicle in which to adjust itself to its new conditions. Besides damaging themselves, unfaithful husbands and wives damage each other, for they steal from the reserve of subtle energy accumulated by marriage.

The negative force of instinct is promiscuity. It is connection with that which is low. Real sex produces a tremendous connection with that which is high. When man and wife are one it is the biggest connection, the biggest act of creation that could take place because it is a pure connection for a real purpose. We have to be pure to create something pure.

Chastity is the careful and constant watch over our physical and spiritual senses, in order to keep them pure and immaculate before God. The married should be careful not to become drunk with the wine of their own barrel.

When we make real connections with people and our influence helps them, if it is a man who does so he becomes more manly and if a woman, she becomes more womanly. A man who helps his wife and children to develop can say: 'This is my wife, these are my children.' A woman who helps her husband and children to develop can say: 'This is my husband, these are my children.' She cannot say that she formed them, but everyone knows it. If we make a real connection with someone, no matter who it is, every influence we put into him is ours, although we cannot say: 'I did it!' We cannot proclaim the fact for others to hear, but we have the internal satisfaction of knowing it. It is a spiritual satisfaction. Each slightest influence lasts; we cannot know how many people we can influence nor how far our influence can reach.

To receive real inspiration it is necessary to purify one's thoughts of everything heavy. It is hard work, but then our mind rises to a point where it can be touched by thought from a higher level. But if our thought is not purified, that which may seem like inspiration will only be imagination.

In a normal, healthy person sex supplies the energy for all creative work. It should flow directly into some creative work without being recognizable as sex energy. Recognizable sex energy is the result of laziness. It means that we have not given ourselves enough work to utilize our creative force. Creative work does not necessarily mean composing music or painting pictures. A housewife who cleans a room is doing creative work, for she is creating order and harmony in her home. It is as important a work as that of an artist, for though the latter may affect a wider immediate range of people, nothing is more intense than the influence of a home. The influence of a woman affects not only her husband and children, but everyone with whom they also come into contact throughout their lives. This is why it is so important that the woman should herself reflect only pure and harmonious influences. She is the selector of the influences that pour onto the home from its surroundings; she selects and reflects those that correspond to her own quality of being.

God created everything clean; it is man who makes things dirty. Adam and Eve were pure because they were made by Christ. The fruit of the tree was dirt. The knowledge of good and evil means that they learnt what was clean and what was dirty. Nothing and nobody can destroy what is pure in us. The light will bring it out and keep it warm. We must never work in the dark. Dirty things are done in the dark, clean things are open.

We must not base our lives on physical things since the result continues after we have left the physical. Spiritualism is criminal for this reason. When anyone who is very attached to his physical body dies, his soul is attracted by its chemical irradiations and stays tied to this level without disintegrating, thus preventing the spirit from being liberated. People who practise spiritualism call these souls and bind them even more firmly to this level by giving them opportunities to manifest themselves. This chains their spirits. The only spirits who can be called to manifest on the physical level are those who are identified with the physical world. They may be identified by a desire to help, not having discovered in this life that no one can help anyone through identification. This accounts for the high moral tone of many spirit messages. Many so-called spirit messages come from the sub-conscious of the medium, and if this is an altruistic person the 'messages' will be elevating in tone. Nine tenths of 'spirit manifestations' are due to trickery, sleight-of-hand, suggestion or hypnotism in one form or another. But in cases of genuine manifestations the only way we can 'prove the spirits' is not, as many people think, by whether their messages are elevating or not, but by whether they have been provoked by seances or mediumship, or whether they have come as a response to prayer to God alone.

Spirits should go up, not be held down. If a spirit is held down, when it goes higher it can get lost. We can help spirits by praying to God for them. Our prayers are food for spirits. We must help them and pray for them but never bring them down. We must not disturb them from the place where they should be.

Only free spirits, saints, higher men, can speak to persons who are still alive. They come as revelations. Real revelations by free spirits are never made in the dark or involve loss of consciousness in the person receiving them. This is why in every religious representation of spirit manifestations the 'vision' is surrounded by a bright light or halo and the person receiving the vision or communication is depicted in a state of heightened consciousness.

There are plenty of low spirits trying to get in touch with people on this earth. They can only do so through the medium of low-level people and *only if they are called*. They do not have permission to do it unless they are called, but because God gave us free will, if we want them and call them they will come. If we call a high spirit or think of one, the thought goes first to God; then, if it is His will, He sends it to the spirit. We can understand this if we think of God as the brain of the universe. In the human body any stimulus is reported to the brain, which then sends out a message to the area which was stimulated and sometimes also to a corresponding area. All thoughts, good or bad, go straight to the mind of God and stay there for ever, to be used for our judgement. All that the human brain receives is stored on the rolls of memory, forming the basis of our subsequent reactions or judgements. Man was formed in the image of God in many more ways than we realize.

Free spirits can go up and down between heaven and earth like the angels in Jacob's dream. How often do we realize that we exist within their consciousness? The fourth dimension interpenetrates the three dimensions[1] in which we have our physical existence, the world of limitation and illusion. The fourth dimension is consciousness, light, reality.[2]

[1] Matter, space and time.
[2] See the introduction to *A New Model of the Universe* by P. D. Ouspensky.

III

There is a work that has had many names. In the first century it was called the Work of Faith, in the twelfth century it was called the Work of Works, in the sixteenth century the Work of Laws, in the eighteenth, the Work of Reason. In our time it should be called the Work of Harmony. It is much greater than any one man's work; it is the work of all the high ones put together. Each contributed something.

Our work is harmony in all things; to be honest, truthful and sincere. Truthfulness must come from us. Sincerity must come from others. Honesty comes from above. Truthfulness is everywhere except in us, so we have to work to gain it. Sincerity must come from others, for we must enable them to be sincere with us. Honesty is from above; it is the strength God gives us. Honesty is consideration and will.

Consideration for others must be our first measure. Consideration is like a plate onto which everything we eat must first be served. To think that others have the same possibilities and the same failings that we have – that is honesty. Being truthful, sincere and honest we become humble, for we realize that we are nothing and at the same time that we have everything.

Sincerity is recognition of our true feelings. This does not mean that we have to disclose them to other people, for often to do so is not honest. Honesty is dealing with people in such a way that we do not hurt them. To hurt people and to hurt their feelings is very different; sometimes we have to hurt their feelings in order not to hurt their selves. Truthfulness is understanding laws and living in accordance with them.

It is necessary to be truthful in order to find the real meaning of things. Only by truthfulness can we find our being or significance. By discovering our own being we can discover the inner sense of everything else. Veracity is the instrument by which we discover higher truth, therefore the way to the truth of life is truthfulness. And then? To know what lies on the level of truthfulness it is necessary to have reached it. We all have powers that we can use when we love the truth.

Our work is so pure that we must free ourselves from this present of material things. We must always try to feel up, in space. When we have that sensation we will never lose it. It is a wonderful work; it fills us with joy. If the work is not joyful it is not right. It is beautiful because it links everything and brings it higher.

The work is the truth; we do not realize how high it is. We are here to give it simply. We still complicate it. Every question is answered in our work; it is simplified for us to understand. If we are open and objective we will see how very simple it is. Work is becoming sensitive to and fulfilling the requirements of ordinary daily life.

There is only one school: the school of truth. Sects use labels because they know only half the truth. The real truth has no name. The truth is in everything. Our work is all religions; it is real understanding. What is the difference between early Christianity and the way today? It is the same. The work cannot be new, but truth must always be expressed in new language. The words of Christ have waited two thousand years to be understood. They can be understood at once with clear thoughts and clean minds. The Gospels were not written only for people two thousand years ago. They are always a new force, and it is our duty to relate the situation of each individual to every passage of the Gospels, interpreting it not only with the mind but with the emotions of our hearts. The work is always there; it cannot change. It is ourselves who must change, to find a way to express it.

Everybody has the truth of God in himself, but the trouble is that everybody believes the truth he sees is the only one. As long as we know that our vision is limited, we see more. Why do people want to impose their ideas on others? They even want to impose their own ideas of taste on others. When we try to force our thoughts onto a person we are not teaching; but if we try to hear what he does not understand, we are learning; then we can feel the person and can teach him. There is only one truth and people must come to it in their own way. If intellectual people are imposed on they go away; if simple people are imposed on they follow blindly, and that is no use either to themselves or to others. If we want to help we must do so; we can teach, help, but not impose.

In order to teach others what to do, we must first know what we should do ourselves. He who does not know how to swim cannot plunge into the water to save others. To teach is to understand, to understand is to accept, to accept is to realize, to realize is to find truth. The mind must be used to find truth in us, not pictures of truth. The way to truth is sincerity and honesty. Truth is recognized by its clarity. Everything confused is a lie. But we have to find truth in that which is confused. Everything true is simple. The simple things are the real ones. We complicate everything to suit our personality, because we think things are too simple for our great minds.

It is enough really to want to be honest, truthful and sincere. If we say we are so, we are judging. But if we want to be so, we are asking for help and we know that help will come. Mankind has always been inspired since the beginning, helped towards its goal. There is a place which echoes that inspiration, but we cannot search for it outside ourselves. It is within that we must look. We must find the place. Then we must give, give and give. What can we give? Faith and constancy.

Our work is to find and help those who do not yet know what harmony means. If we give truth and sincerity those who want it will hear. Millions of people everywhere are waiting, asking for truth. They feel it, smell it. They will come. We must not be discouraged because of those who do not come, for we have no right to impose anything on anybody. We must be tolerant and kind to everyone; it is our obligation. Our real work is with patience, tolerance and constancy.

People come to us hoping that we will tell them what in their hearts they already know. If we let them talk they will say what that is and see it clearly for themselves. If we tell them our own ideas we will be telling them what we need, not what they need, and they will be disappointed. The right way to help them is to tell them what they want, to give them confidence so that they will find for themselves what they must do. We will never know what people are if we do not observe what they say. If we think: 'I have to listen to them' we will never know. If we think: 'What are they trying to tell me?' then we will know.

We can say so much by one word. One word has many meanings. We can make people happy with a word and hurt people by a word. We must never tell a person what he really is – only what he is pretending to be, or is not. No one can trespass; what a person is in himself is sacred.

We must talk in a way that everyone can understand. When we talk with people we must work very fast. We must get used to feeling whether or not they are ready for what we want to say, whether they can accept it at that moment or whether it will do harm to say it. When we want to say something we must ask ourselves: 'Is this honest? Do I really know his state of mind at this moment?' It may be sincere to speak sharply to someone, but if we feel that he will resent it we are not being honest if we speak to him in such a way. When we want to help others and know at the same time that it might disturb them, we must forget ourselves and speak to them for their sake only.

It is true that we must render good for evil, but nevertheless we must be careful not to give too much to those who have done us wrong, because if we do so we harm them by making them believe it is our obligation to do them good. It is not an obligation. We can meet everyone, but it does not mean that we must invite everybody to live in our house. We must help people with pure feeling, but it does not mean that we must be sympathetic. Nobody grows by apparent kindness, for that makes people weak. Real kindness is when we push people upwards. They may call it roughness. How often we scold our children, then go out and laugh. But what good would it do them, when they have done something wrong, to make them feel we were pleased with them? That would not be real kindness. To them, our scolding was not kindness; from our point of view it was, but from theirs it was not.

We must be alert all the time. If a person cannot digest more knowledge it is no use giving him any more. But if the next person is hungry we must give him what he needs. When we want to give someone an idea we must know how prepared he is. If we are going to plant a seed we must know if the land is fertilized or not. If it is not, we have to fertilize it first.

We see someone pass; we must give him understanding. It is easy enough to give him money or an old coat. Desire to help others grows by seeing their need. When we really see their need, then we cannot but long to help. We must work to be attuned to others. If we rest in other people's words we can help them. When we talk to people we must try to give them the impression that everything we say comes from them. We must never impose, never command, never force. If we feel that something is needed and try to give it, that is different. Love is the only power that can make help real.

People do not understand each other. They do not see that they are all the same – all passing through the same difficulties, problems, diseases. Nobody is any better, nobody is any worse. We all have to pass through it all. We are all balanced the same. Everything we give we will receive. In the way we give, in that way we will receive. If we respect others they will respect us, if we understand others they will understand us. Everything we give we collect – the same size, the same colour, the same quality. We have to learn to give and take. It is more difficult to take than to give, but we have to learn.

Every contact should be a bargain. If we smile at someone and he smiles back it is a bargain. It is the same with being sincere. We have to be honest in these bargains; we should be very careful to weigh them, but we do not, because we waste so much time thinking of ourselves. We can help when we are sincere, when we say what we really know. If we know more than others it will help them, if we know less it will help them too. To help is a cycle; we can only help people if they help us. We must all work, work with love, work with harmony. But it has to be real harmony, not just words, not by preaching but by action. To love our neighbour is easy, but to make our neighbour love us, to act so that he can love us, is not at all easy.

We cannot give till we have. Harmony is peace. We must feel peace in order to give it. We have not only to work spiritually but in every way that is needed. We must love, and love rightly and simply. It is not enough for one man to show love; many must show it. And how can we show what we have not got? That is why we must forget ourselves and give. We must not think about ourselves, about whether we are saying the right thing. We can be more open to people by thinking of *them*. We must feel them, feel what they need. There is a master-key that will open everyone: kindness, just kindness.

It is not our fault if we do not understand other people's points of view, but we have to respect them. We must be kind and tolerant with everyone. That is our duty, our real work. There is always something right, good and clean in everyone. We must find it but not force it. We must try to bring it out. The only way to bring out the good in people is by not thinking of ourselves. We must remember that our work is to bring out the best in everything. If we are positive everything surrounding us can be used for that.

Where there is argument there are idiots. The wise man gives his wisdom little by little and if it is not accepted, becomes silent.

We have to accept our neighbour's mistakes in order to be able to accept our own. For example, a wife who sees the mistakes and faults of her husband has to accept them because they are in her, in her imagination. Perhaps they are not faults at all, but something very big that she does not understand. God gave him to her that they might go through everything together. If there are mistakes it is not his fault nor her fault. She must help him go out into life by accepting him as he is, with all his defects, in order to accept herself as she is. We must accept everyone, accept them with our hearts. Villon said: 'This is my monarchy: I have swallowed all my shame.' He had accepted himself. That is the sly man's pill. The greatest happiness is acceptance. It is to be so humble that nothing that is said, no criticism or praise, can hurt us. To be able to accept everything with humility, that is the greatest happiness.

We must make everything our own. If a husband is annoyed with his wife and she makes his annoyance hers, accepts it, they become closer. If he shows her affection and she makes that her own, the same thing happens. We cannot judge, for we do not know what is good or bad. If we make everything of others ours we will be happy; no one can take it from us because it will be ours, we will have made it ours. We will be able to do everything, for we will be near God.

We should never go to sleep until we have forgiven everybody, even our own temptations, even ourselves. We must always go to bed clean by forgiveness. When we die we shall not be with the saints and angels; we shall be with the people we have forgiven and who have forgiven us. Where there is pardon there is love. Forgiveness is humility. Where there is humility there is love. Where there is love there is no condemning, because we feel there is nothing to forgive.

Remorse and love are the same. Remorse is real love, or rather love is the pleasure, remorse the pain. If we are really awake we feel remorse in proportion to the injury we have done others; it is payment.

When there is separation there is no knowledge. Civilization grows when people combine in order to see what is lacking and to provide it according to each other's needs. Now there is no civilization because people combine to harm each other.

If we act in accordance with a role we will not hurt anyone. For instance, when a painter comes to teach us and says it is useful to hold the brush in a certain way and that the principal lines should go in such and such a way, he is acting in a role towards us and we will not be hurt by anything he says. Then afterwards we paint our picture ourselves. When we talk and exchange ideas it is in order that we may all grow. If I am wrong tell me so; if you are wrong let us discuss that too. Between our wrong ideas and our right ideas we will come nearer the truth. We must learn not to take discussions personally. When we are talking together we must be like chess-players, watching for opportunities to learn, watching which move will teach us best. We must avoid being personal and hurt if people do not agree with us, for if we are, we are tying ourselves down, making ourselves terreneal, earthly. If we are really positive in learning we feel much better than if we reject our opportunities.

We may feel that we are not helping someone, but how do we know if we are or not? Even if we cannot think of anything to say, how do we know that our smile, the projection of our longing to help, just listening with attention, is not help? It is help. Probably when we can think of nothing to say, when we feel most helpless, we are helping most. For then we pray to Our Lord to help through us. When we talk with a person and do not know what to say, it is not the language in any sense that matters; it is not even experience of what he thinks or how he lives, but the real feelings we have for him that matter. Results will come when we have been open and giving of our real self. When we have felt a tremendous longing to help other people, no matter how, and then have forgotten ourselves, afterwards they may tell us that they have been helped, although we may not remember what we said and feel that we did nothing. Even if we do not understand someone, but think: 'This person needs something; what can I give him?' we have already given him love. And there is nothing that real love does not cure. We cannot tell what people need. We cannot know how we can help people. But if we give positiveness we will help in a way we will never know.

We can collect material things, but we cannot collect love. If we receive it we have to give it again. Many people say they are tired of giving. We all want to receive. We all say that we have given and not received, instead of saying that we have received and so must give. In harmony there is no discontent. Harmony is perfect freedom. Real freedom is real love. Love is liberty. When we demand we do not love. Nobody in real work demands anything for himself. Always beware of those who demand for themselves, no matter what reason they give.

In this world no one can become perfectly selfless, but when we are really strong, really ourselves, and help others, then we are near selflessness.

Nothing is done by ourselves; others help us in everything we do. When we understand that we have to help other people, give to other people, then we are safe, for we are already stamped with what we have to be. The divine in us wants to become what it is supposed to be. The divine in us realizes itself in wanting to help others, and this is love.

IV

Nothing belongs to us except the love of God. If we have that, we have won it for ourselves by loving our neighbour. Everything else is lent to us to use for others. Even the food we eat goes to make our blood, which together with oxygen creates the irradiations which go to other people. For this reason we have to take care of our things so that when someone else needs them they may be available. We shall have to give account for everything we have not taken care of. We have the obligation to require of others that they respect our things in the same way that we respect them.

If we arrange our house for ourselves, saying: 'This is *my* house?' it will not be arranged right. But if we remember our responsibility, that we have to project something, give something through the impression that our house gives to those who come into it, our house will be arranged with good taste. We have to connect everything. If we want our house to be harmonious we have to connect the things in it with their purpose and with their surroundings.

The key to everything we do is attention to the intention. Then the smallest detail will be right both in relation to our physical surroundings and our actions. Then we will never do anything to impress. 'Let not thy left hand know what thy right hand doeth' means if we do something good we should do it for the sake of the good and not that men may say that we are good. Everything must be done from the heart, sincerely. Because God knows all that is hidden and from Him alone we will have our reward. If we do something good and tell about it, we have lost it; anyone might have done it and we reap no benefit. If we try to keep something for ourselves we lose it. This applies to everything, including money. We only have money if we spend it, for money in itself is worthless. But it must be spent wisely. We have no right to waste it, because our money does not belong to us any more than anything else.

If we really belong to this work we do nothing for ourselves and nothing belongs to us. Everything we have belongs to God, to God's work. When we know that, we are free. Freedom means belonging to God.

If we wash our bodies, it is not for ourselves; it is because our instruments have to be kept clean for God's work. We have to keep our bodies biologically clean, and that is not for ourselves either, but for God's work, since our bodies belong to God. We should look after our bodies, remembering that they are sacred, that they may serve God. If one has an illness it is an obligation to try to cure it and if it is not cured, accept it.

Asceticism can be of different kinds; it can be a sacrifice to God, with pure intention, or it can be through hate of oneself, which is a vice. There is so much suffering in this world as it is, that needs to be absorbed, that to want to create suffering for oneself is unbalanced. There is negative suffering and positive suffering. Positive suffering is to absorb the mechanical suffering of others, take it so effectively that they do not have it. Negative suffering involves further suffering by others in one form or another and always results from psychological sleep. Positive suffering implies a level of consciousness on which negative suffering cannot exist. Pain lies between negative and positive suffering and can be absorbed by either.

'Leave thy body and come' does not mean that we have to forget the body. We must make good use of it but remember that we have to leave it. The body will take us to God or prevent us from going to Him, depending on the use we make of it. People who voluntarily suffer pain do so in order to put the physical body in its proper place and rise above it. In order to stand the pain they have to be on a higher level. Liberty means making the body obey the spirit. God is not displeased when we try to obtain benefits for the body as long as those benefits are placed at the service of the spirit.

Sacrifice does not mean giving up something one likes in order to please God; it means getting rid of the false. The reason why many people are fascinated with the idea of sacrifice is because they confuse it with mechanical suffering, which they are not willing to sacrifice. They would have to admit that it was nothing praiseworthy, but on the contrary simply the result of sleep.

How little we think about death or what is going to happen to us after death. We know quite well we are not going to take this body with us, so we should think about the part of us that will go on after death. Our body is not nearly as important a part of us as our soul, yet we take care to feed our body. If we feed our body that when we die is only going to feed worms, how much more should we feed our soul, to enable it to be strong when it leaves the body.

Everything real begins from something real, but imagination corrupts reality. Imagination plays a very strong part in the physical body. If we imagine we are tired, we *are* tired. We must remember the part the mind plays in the actions of the physical body, especially in sex. We should not confuse real emotions with imaginary emotions.

People often study, then add imagination to what they have learned. If a person has really believed for a long time that he will see a doll walking, in time he will come to see it. If we have prejudice, have already imagined what we will see, then we cannot be open. We must be open, otherwise our imagination holds our prejudices and preconceptions round us. They stick to us and we will see our imaginations and never be able to see real things.

There are three kinds of imagination – negative, mechanical and positive. Negative imagination is day-dreaming about something that has no possibility of being put into fact. Mechanical imagination is making an image of something automatic that we are going to do, such as driving a car. Unless we imagined it first we could not do it; we can make no intentional move-ment unless we imagine it first. Positive imagination is creative, as when a painter imagines the picture he is going to paint – and paints it. If he does not paint it he was day-dreaming and his imagination was negative.

47

We can control our feelings by connection. We can make our circumstances, and feelings come by connection with circumstances. Many of our feelings are brought by ourselves, by what we choose to think about. There are always many kinds of feelings in us; which we recognize, which we encourage, is for us to choose. We must not lose by laughter what we have gained by tears.

It is difficult to generalize about feelings, for they depend on sensitiveness. There are people who can burn their fingers and not feel anything; others have only to hear fire spoken of and they feel burned. Many feelings are caused by imagination. Feelings are functions. If the organ is clean the function is clean. The organ is the container for something given from above.

'I' is a sacred word. Usually we mean 'us' – a whole row of 'I's'. We must learn to put them on shelves. One 'I' feels something; if we say to ourselves: 'That "I" feels such and such', it is as though we put it on its shelf. Another 'I' feels something and we put it on *its* shelf. When people keep talking about their 'I's' they do not grow. With 'I said this', 'I showed that', 'I did the other' we will never grow. If a drop of water falls into the sea, is it the drop which gives its name to the sea or the sea to the drop of water?

Vanity is negative. If we recognize something positive we have done and are vain about it, the positiveness is lost. But if, when we recognize that we have done something positive, we immediately think of using it for others, we continue turning it into positiveness. When we attempt to do something - say write something – for ourselves, for our own pleasure or vanity, inevitably something goes wrong, something is wrong with it. But when we try to do something for the sake of others, write down something that it may be available for others, then we are open and receive help.

When we do something good we should ask ourselves why. When we do something wrong we know it. It is when we do something good that we have to be alert, because we often do what appears to be good through self-righteousness or vanity. We can do everything with vanity or without vanity. There can be vanity in our recognition of our obligations to others. Even if we work for money that is not for ourselves but for others, it can be for vanity. Many people with money are not real; they want to make themselves out to be what they are not. Their mind does not go with their circumstances. They travel but do not know how to find, because they do not know how to be alone. We notice nothing that goes on around us if we are resting on the feathers of our vanity. We all feel very lonely sometimes – by vanity only. For we are not alone in anything. If we loved others and understood them we would never feel lonely.

To ourselves we feel very important. We think: 'I want.' If we felt our real positions then things would come to us. We should let them be and not try to hold them. If we forget ourselves things will come to us. Self-importance is always binding us, hindering us in everything. We must break the chain of our importance. He who thinks himself important has no importance; he who thinks himself completely unimportant begins to have importance. We should never remember that we are 'James' or 'John', only that we are 'we'. Then we will never be embarrassed, for embarrassment is false personality. We should be very careful not to be embarrassed, because it is vanity. It is imagination and an old habit.

Most of our fears come from vanity. We fear that others will find us stupid, that they will understand more than we do. We can understand anything, if we are willing to study.

Everyone has a mental picture of himself. When we see ourselves in a photograph or a mirror we say: 'I am really better than that!' We take ourselves very seriously. If we forgot ourselves a little we would have some knowledge.

Worry is the worst prejudice we have, because it comes from vanity. Bad temper is a compound of vanity and imagination. We get cross with circumstances because we cannot cope with them. We get cross when we do not want to make an effort to cope with them.

Vanity is our worst enemy. Vanity does nothing for the thing itself, but for the effect it will have on others. When we cease to think of ourselves, of what impression we give, then we will be free. When we are thinking of other people, not of ourselves, the rest will take care of itself. When we learn to listen to others and forget ourselves, then we already are something. We think that to forget ourselves means giving up something pleasant. We do not realize that to do so means entering into a new state of happiness.

Everyone is basically alike. We all have the same problems; they all come from vanity. We know the cause, but many do not. They feel that the illusion is really true and we know it is not true.

Tolerance kills vanity. Tolerance does not mean condoning things that seem to us to be wrong. It means not reacting mechanically to them. If we face everything in ourselves and do not make excuses, then we are tolerant. If we make excuses we are reacting to the unpleasant things we see in ourselves.

To speak of mysticism in order to impress, to speak for the sake of speaking, is as bad as prostitution. We should ask ourselves every day why we are here, why we have been given this responsibility, why we meet together, why we are connected so strongly. It is a grace that we are together, that we are in the Work, the Work of Works.

The Work is in each one of us, in himself. Many people think they are in the work who do not understand it. Others supposedly not in the work have always been in it. We are not in the work yet; we have not begun. There are many people in the work, but they are invisible. If someone really and truly is in the work he is invisible.

We can understand the opposite of vanity if we think about the process of blending tobacco. A blend has a better flavour than any one of its components. Each individual loses its own particular flavour and acquires the better flavour of the whole. If we really understand this we may feel a pang at realizing that our 'I' has to die in order that the greater I, which is included in 'we', may be born. Only our intelligence can tell us that this is wholly desirable, that nothing real will be lost, that on the contrary illusions and imaginations prevent us from experiencing a happiness far greater than any possible for our many and petty 'I's'. The greatest happiness we can experience on this earth comes from humility so complete that nothing said to us or about us can make us react either with pleasure or with pain. When we accept whatever comes to us as an opportunity to learn, as an opportunity for being positive, then we will be really happy. When that point of humility is reached there is no longer 'I want', there is only 'we are'. This is self-remembering.

Blessed are the pure of heart; blessed are the humble; blessed be those who speak the word of God; blessed be those who are united in the name of the Lord; blessed be those who leave fears and vanities.

V

Religion is a virtue to bring us near Our Lord; a science to strengthen will. It is a science of many things. It is love, it is self-remembering. It is to be able to see from outside to inside. It is not a word which we can understand in our imagination; we must practise it by loving people. We must lay down our imagination and practise religion by being truthful, honest and sincere.

Religion is connection with God by ethics. Our conscience tells us not to hurt other people. That is religion. We may not talk of God, but if we live by ethics we are religious. Harmony and beauty go by taste into ethics.

Taste can be developed with attention and knowledge. Many circumstances can develop taste. A person with good taste will never sin. When we have taste we want to learn and go by the highest to perfection. We give the exact value to everything – we see things as they are. We learn how to measure. We measure our words and have taste because we do not condemn. When we have taste we are living outside ourselves, seeing, hearing, touching everything. We are really living. We are no longer in imagination because there is no more exaggeration. We are balanced.

The better taste we have, the better conscience we have. Conscience is a faculty possessed by everyone, but we must realize that there are undeveloped consciences. If we feel something is honest we should do it. What was honest a month ago may be dishonest today, because our conscience is developing. Conscience is the best faculty we have. Everyone has the same conscience, but in some people it is more developed than in others. For instance, one person may think it is dishonest to cheat by a shilling but not by a penny; to another it may be dishonest to cheat by a farthing, because his conscience is more developed. The only way we can develop our conscience is by wisdom. Understanding is like light; it is a very big word – it means knowledge, tolerance, conscience, wisdom.

Wisdom is understanding how to turn circumstances so that they are useful. Facing them makes us grow – facing them with everything that is in us, looking with both eyes. Usually we look at things with one eye only; prejudice makes us shut the other.

We are more clean when we have temptations. When we notice that our hands are dirty we wash them; then they are cleaner than they were before. No one is ever free from temptations. A man reaches the level of divinity by the force of the human world. Blessed are temptations, because they make us strong.

We should face our responsibilities, take our responsibilities. Responsibility is like a string of which we can see only the middle; both ends are out of sight. The man who is reliable in small things is reliable in big things. If someone says he will post a letter for you and does not do it, no matter for what reason, he has shown himself to be unfitted for responsibility of any kind. If we cannot be trusted with the little things of this world, how can we be trusted with celestial treasures?

One of the most important things for us is consistency. If we were consistently good we could be used as instruments; if we were consistently bad we could be used also, in a different way. But we are unreliable. We can be useful to others if we know how to say clearly what we think. A person who can express himself clearly thinks clearly. A person who thinks clearly acts consistently. If people say they feel but cannot express what it is they feel, they are not feeling but identifying themselves with it.

We have to do right in all conditions. We have to do our best. If we are doing right we should never feel hurt. If we are not doing right, not doing the work of Our Lord, then we should feel hurt. We must not imagine we are hurt when we are not. Let the small things be small and the big things big.

We must not do good that looks bad nor wrong that looks right. We must try everything, think, accept, think for ourselves, measure for ourselves, eliminate what we do not think is right.

Consciousness and conscience are the same. Consciousness is awareness of our surroundings and of ourselves in them. Conscience is awareness of the effects of our actions on our surroundings. It is alertness to right and wrong. Alertness, awareness, both mean being awake, remembering oneself. Conscience is alertness of mind, of the three parts of the mind that come together in us and make consciousness. Conscience is incorruptible, the best that we have. It is the continuity of this life to eternity. It means thinking, projecting. We are not here to do anything physically; we have to develop our minds. That makes us grow spiritually. We must develop our minds, for the more developed the mind the more developed the conscience. If we use our minds there is nothing in this world that we cannot understand – if we have the will to discover it.

We have a conscience and a will. Conscience may tell us not to do this or that, but without will we cannot obey it. Will introduces conscience into thought. As we are, what we do is predetermined, but if we acquire will, what we do is not predetermined. Our physical movements are predetermined; if we walk it is predetermined that we move first one foot and then another. If we decide to sit, it is predetermined that we bend our knees. If we are dirty it is predetermined that we will continue to be dirty until we make an effort to be clean and predetermine that we will be clean. We control our breathing by a clean mind. If our conscience is dirty we are disturbed and our breathing becomes disturbed.

Conscience is the voice of the spirit. The recognition of conscience is in the soul. The body cannot recognize conscience because it is physical. The bridge between conscience and the body is recognition, soul. The soul accepts, looks. If we see something beautiful and realize it, that is the operation of the soul. That is self-remembering. It is necessary always to make the connection between spirit and body, otherwise we just exist without being.

The first step is to know that we *are*, that we have a mind. The second is to have a conscience, to acknowledge conscience. The third is to know our aim. The fourth is to know ourselves and to be humble. That is real self-remembering. At first we can be guided, but after the first or second step we ourselves have to decide whether we will go up or down. For God has given us free will and even He Himself cannot compel us to go in any direction. We ourselves have to decide. We have constantly to make decisions because we lack will and a permanent centre of gravity. Our possibilities are the greatest assets we have. In order for them to be realized we must not strengthen our weaknesses.

Every action without will is negative. There is only one will; it is like a light that we must always follow; it has to be vibrating all the time. We make it by wanting it. Will is essential for everyone. Without it we can go nowhere. With will we can make ourselves *be*. Nobody can give us will but ourselves. Since God gave us free will even He cannot touch it. Free will means the ability to choose whether or not to exercise what little will we have. Spirit and body do not belong to us, but the soul does, because it is will. The only thing that really belongs to us is our will.

Everyone has a will, although we may think we have none. An action is brought to completion by one of two causes; either the impulse which started it is strong enough to carry it through, or we have sufficient strength of will to do so. We are constantly completing actions by our own will, but they are so small and insignificant compared to the actions completed by the strength of the original impulse that we do not notice them. Further, we are much more apt to notice the instances where our will was not sufficiently strong to complete an action than those in which it was strong enough to do so.

Will is the strongest thing there is – the right will. We cannot be perfect; that is impossible. But we have to be strong. We have the key: honesty, truthfulness and sincerity.

The way to be alive is to help others to be alive. If we forget ourselves in order to help others we have attention. Attention necessitates will. Ourself and the object of our attention are two factors; will is the third. When the three factors come together the result is we are more live, we are ourselves, we have being.

We can lose our being through the habit of mechanicalness. If the will is attached to the body, our being becomes less. Will has to obey our being and not the body. If we act from being we act rightly, but if our 'I's' get in the way we are not right. We can make our essence grow and develop our being. If we have being we have soul, because with being we have will. It is the work of the will to make essence reach being. By will we can develop greater being than that with which we were born. We feed the seed of essence with little wishes until they become desire. Whatever we want we get. If we *really* want to be clean we will be, in that instant.

We have every possibility. Everything is there if we want it with the real centre of ourselves – not the left side, not the right side, but the real centre of ourselves. We can do everything by will. If we have will we have grace. We can do anything by ourselves, by effort. Not, of course, on a physical level; for example, if we do not eat we have no strength in our minds.

The word 'difficult' should not exist in our vocabulary. Immediately it introduces imagination and limits us. Nothing is difficult. There is nothing difficult for the human being. Every possibility is in us, only we say: 'Oh, no, that is impossible!' To be transformed we must stop thinking of 'buts'. So many things in our lives are 'but – but – but'. If we stop saying 'but' we will be ourselves.

We must try by will to collect more will. We must not just worry about it. By worrying we limit ourselves. We are the ones who limit ourselves. We are all in the same position. Worrying helps nothing; it means that we are uncertain. Nothing right can come of it, for it closes our sense perceptions. Exaggeration by worry brings instability. We have tremendous possibilities, with no limitations except those we impose on ourselves. We must break these limitations. We are the image of God. We are unaware of it; that is why we limit ourselves. God made us in His image to be free, to be clean, to be happy. Because God made us in His image we can do everything. We make things wrong by limiting ourselves.

The only way to be really happy is to be really free, and the only way to be really free is not to have imaginary fears. Fears are only imaginary, never real. They are outside us, not inside. It is we who build up imaginary things to fear. Imagination is very fast. It is imagination that brings fear. Immediately we must say: 'I have will power and I am going to project something real. There is nothing to be frightened of; this is a waste of energy.' Will power is completely effective against imagination; just will.

Each morning we should set ourselves an aim for the day, a particular aim, and try with all our strength to realize it. We may forget it after an hour, we may forget it after ten minutes. But if for ten minutes each day we really tried to carry out our own aim we set ourselves, then we would be making something of our own that nobody could take away from us. Then we would go forward.

To examine our conscience does not mean to try to score up against ourselves all the times we have failed to carry out our aim. That only increases our self-importance. To examine our conscience means to go through the day and see how many people have taught us something, to how many people we should be grateful. To say: 'What have I done wrong?' is to think of oneself. Think of 'them', not 'I'. 'I' is worth nothing. But the aggregate of 'I' and 'them' is worth something.

There are three stages in this work: surprise, fear and understanding. Surprise is the delight we feel at finding something new. We have fear when we see that we have to give up all human feelings – frictions, worries, prejudices; fear of really recognizing the truth, of having to kill the wrong 'I' – '*I* like, *I* need.' Understanding is knowing what is our real 'I'. To realize harmony we must forget personality and think only of cause and effect. He fulfils himself who in the highest possible degree fits his word with his thoughts, harmonizes his thoughts with his conduct and conforms his conduct with the intimate reality of man.

VI

If we find peace in ourselves we will be at peace with heaven and earth. Real happiness is to be free – on a higher level than that which we usually call happiness. We call many things suffering because they last longer than happiness, which goes fast. Much of the time we think we are happy because our bodies feel well; for instance, if we have had a toothache and it stops, we think we are happy. Pain exists only in the non-existent. Sadness and happiness are much the same – a circle. Freedom and happiness are again a circle, only a higher one. We cannot be ourselves on a low level; to be ourselves we have to be on a high level. We must not be attached to things inside time, but to things that are out of time. We have to work for out of time.

Our work is in time; we can choose whether to take it slowly or to hurry. This is not a work for a few months. It is for ever. Once we really enter the work we cannot go back. Those who stop on the way are immediately lost and unhappy. They have nothing to hold to any more. They cannot go back to where they were before. As long as we are occupied, looking and moving forward in this work, we are happy. As soon as we fall back there is great suffering. And the further we have gone the more painful and terrible it is to fall. For that reason it is never right to urge people too much at the beginning. People with energy and determination always want special conditions, special exercises. The problem is that they can manage them once, even get interesting results, but they cannot do it again. Then they become disappointed and lose faith. If a person leaves the work it does not only mean that he goes out of it. It means that he changes the work to suit his own ideas.

We all have a rôle to play. There is nothing really frightening but this – to let our chances go, our real time. Time is opportunity. We are given so much time, just so many years. In that time we can do something, make something. If we do not use this time there is no other. Opportunity is coincidence – the way into higher worlds. It means our own inner possibility concurring with the possibility provided from a higher level. Real time is when everything is clear and possible for us. Then we must use it. We must not go back. We must gain time, not kill it. We must use it by acting towards other people according to the possibilities of the time. Everyone has a kairos time, when great things are possible for him, only he does not know when it is. If only people understood about kairos time it would make them stay alert always because they never know when it is coming. Kairos time is the proof of unlimitation.

We should be aware of all the processes, watch everything moving in us, be aware of every movement. 'When the eyes are shut the windows are shut; when the mouth is shut the door is shut; when the heart is closed the door is closed.' When the mouth is shut is when we do not know how to express what we know.

How do we know that we are alive? Not by consciousness, because that does not die. But we can tell by mind that we are alive. We must learn what it is to feel, to give and collect at the same time. We must feel ourselves alive, feel everything living around us, really feel it; feel that we are alert, feel ourselves a fragment of our surroundings. This is another meaning of self-remembering – to remember that greater self of which our own self is but a tiny part, in fact as zero to infinity. That is why to remember ourselves means to forget ourselves, to shift our gaze from one factor of a dimension to the dimension as a whole, where there is no separation between the component parts. For when we say 'myself', we usually mean 'myself-but-not-you'.

We must feel what we can see and touch, but recognize that they are fragments only, because we cannot feel all. Why cannot we always see the colours in everything, really see things? The problem is to be alive. When we are alive we see and hear. We are alive when we connect our eyes with our real 'I'. Then we connect our 'I's' with our real 'I'. We do not do it because we have the habit of laziness. To do it requires will; to do it requires the development of will, little by little, day by day. We develop will by bringing our attention to the intention of whatever we are doing at the moment. But we do not do this because we are lazy and excuse our laziness by saying that we have no will. Consciousness is a deed with attention.

No one can eat our food for us. Everyone can tell us of beautiful things, but until we kill our ignorance and find them for ourselves we will not see them. We develop only by diminishing our ignorance. Ignorance obscures everything, makes it negative. It is our greatest enemy.

We have to digest everything. We have to combine emotions, logic and psychology. We must go step by step to the inner part, and it is emotion that connects all parts together. We have to understand everything that is on this level. If we do not understand things on this level we cannot expect to understand those of a higher level. If we do not break prejudices we will not understand things that are on this level. First we have to reach a logical mind and then a psychological mind. We have to go through logic and un-logic, go through them and be free of them so we can go to the next phase, Logic is putting thoughts into words. We have come to think of logic as reason, but it is not; it is the science of *speaking* reasonably.

Psychology is the knowledge of the soul. Logical mind recognizes the psychological, psychological mind recognizes the esoteric. When the mind includes the heart, then it is psychological, because heart and mind have been harmonized. If this does not seem logical we must remember that it was not by logic that America was discovered, for by logic no one could suppose that a continent existed where people walked with their feet upwards. It was not by logic that the planets were discovered, for not by logic could men have known that there were stones in the heavens. It was by something in their hearts. All discoveries have been made by something in men's hearts.

We think we know, but we know nothing. The day

we accept the fact that we know nothing, we will have wisdom. We are all on the same level of ignorance. None of us knows where others are wrong. We have to accept them as they are in order to accept ourselves as we are. Then we shall have understanding and wisdom and love – or rather charity, which is the approach to love.

That which we transform with love we can project to others and so help them without criticism. If we just say someone's name with feeling we help them. Logic and feeling together is something real. We have reached the psychological level when we know that everything we do by ourselves is not enough. When we try to describe a miracle with logic it is no longer a miracle. It is the same with mysteries; they cannot be described logically, only psychologically. And a secret is a secret only as long as it is kept; as soon as it is divulged it is not a secret.

If we are told to do something, we must *think*. This is real self discipline; to verify, to make ourselves find seven or more reasons why a thing is right or not right. If we cannot find them it is because we have not learned to think quickly. If we have read a book and only learned it by heart we have not assimilated it. If we limit ourselves to words we will never progress.

To receive real inspiration it is necessary to purify one's thoughts of everything heavy. It is hard work, but then our mind rises to a point where it can be touched by thought from a higher level. But if our thought is not purified, that which may seem like inspiration will only be imagination.

Thoughts are a grace; they are given. The mind is like a cup into which water is poured from above. If the cup is clean the water is clean. We can make our container better. If our cup is copper, we can make it silver; if it is silver, we can make it gold.

We can make energy by having pure thoughts. But we must not fight bad thoughts. Everything we do has its repercussions and bad thoughts are repercussions from things we did in the past that we have grown out of doing. Everything has its repercussions, but they are not real. We must not fight things that are unreal; it is a waste of energy. There is a very simple way of getting rid of negative thoughts – just by thinking of harmonious colours.

If we concentrate our thoughts sufficiently strongly on another person it affects him. For instance, if for a certain reason we concentrate on a person the thought that he is going to drop something he is holding, he will drop it. He may think we have supernatural powers. It is only that we have the quite natural power of concentration. The trouble is we do not develop this natural power.

In order to concentrate, in order to be able to project our thoughts to other people, we have to be harmonized ourselves. That means we have to know that we are doing right, that we have the right motive for doing it. If we have any doubts at all, if even a tiny part of our conscience is in doubt that we are doing it in order to help the other person, we are not harmonized, we are not acting as a whole. And if there is any division in us we cannot be concentrated and so have no power of projection; our thoughts are not projected, they are just diffused.

We make what we think. The mind is very strong; it is the strongest part of us. The thoughts that we feed come alive. If we want to go higher we have to go through where we are now. So we must feed nothing but clear thoughts, so that our minds will be clean, with the thoughts that our conscience tells us are clean. Thus we shall live in reality and truth. We must not permit a dark thought to stay in our mind, because dark thoughts are dead and if we do not feed them we will not have to pass through dead moments. We must not criticize nor say anything of others that we have not made our own, made our own by clear thoughts in a clean mind.

Concentration is a sense which prepares for thought. Reason is the container of thoughts. We should listen with logic, feeling and intellect harmonized by attention. The truth in ourselves is real feeling complemented by logic. To learn is to enter into the new. Often what we take to be thoughts are only a collection of mental impressions. Real thoughts are creative.

New things can only come from ourselves. A change of level can only come from ourselves. We cannot be told anything new because we would not hear it. We have to have it already in ourselves in order to hear it.

There are seven circles in learning. The first is that of a very little child who sees the world without realizing that it has to learn anything. The second is when the child is learning the alphabet. The third is when we have learned to read. The fourth is when we realize that there are other people who can teach us besides our mother. The fifth is when we see the difference between teachers. The sixth is when we choose what we want to learn and choose our teacher. The seventh is when we become interested in philosophy. After that we must find everything in ourselves; we realize that we cannot learn from any teacher. The only teacher is God. When we know that, we are shepherds. Up to then we are sheep. Many people never reach even the fifth circle. When we have passed through the seventh circle there is neither good nor bad for us. We do things because it is our duty to do them, not from likes. On that level the only thing that counts is serving our neighbour – nothing else. When we consider people we see their characteristics but we no longer say: 'That is good – that is bad.' We just see people as they are without judging as to whether or not they *ought* to be so. When we have reached that level we know that for us there can be no human teacher. We receive everything direct.

People go from one teacher to another, from one school to another, because they do not put together for themselves by themselves the different parts that the first school gave them. Of course they go from one to another because the whole is not given them. Only by themselves, looking up but not looking down, can they grow. We must look down to help but not to be helped. Everything that is ours has to be won with effort. By that means it belongs to us and no one can take it away from us.

All work must be for ourselves; it must pass through

us for us to give out again in irradiations. It is our business to digest, to work by ourselves with enthusiasm, with love, with dedication. If we do not understand we cannot digest. Our job is to raise ourselves, to connect with the high, so that we can be used.

Love is real humility. Obedience is the greatest grace of humanity; it is all love. Humility, love and obedience are the three forces that, brought together, make grace. There is nothing we cannot do by obedience. If we were really obedient someone could say to us: 'Write a poem!' and we could write a poem. We could be told: 'Dance!' and we would dance even though we had never danced before. Obedience means hearing.

There is nothing mysterious anywhere. What appears to be magic, when people do things or have powers that appear to be supernatural, is only that they can see more than we can, just simply notice more than we notice. Then they can do more than we can do. If you really notice someone else, notice his face, his expression, his movements, the lines round his eyes, the way he sits, the way he moves his hands, you will see what he is. You may say to him: 'You are thinking so and so, you have such and such a difficulty', and he may think you are clairvoyant. But it is simply that you notice him. Everything we do and think has to come out, show itself in some way or other. Drops of water may be seeping into a wall; at a certain moment they have to come out. One person will notice that the wall is damp, another will not.

We have great wisdom that could be developed if

we could lose our mechanicalness. But we lose ourselves through abstract memory. This is memory unconnected with anything real. We can use our memories if we understand things, feel them and sense them.

What is life? To see the consequences of our actions. We really possess that which we accept consciously. To accept consciously is to understand.

Our work is real understanding, to prepare for peace. The gift of understanding enlightens us. It throws a living, penetrating and extraordinary light upon revealed truths. It brings to us a sure means of knowing the real meaning of the divine word.

VII

There are so many grand things to think about there is no time to be muddled, there is no time to think about ourselves. We must think: 'I am doing this for those who are to come.' Then our thinking is unlimited. But if we think of ourselves and say: 'What have I done! What mistakes I have made!' we limit ourselves. We must not be limited. We must realize that we are instruments and that there is no limit to what can be done through us if we do not think it is ourselves who are doing.

None of our errors have killed us. If we take them to learn from it is good. Ignorance means that the light has not come to us. Sleep means that we have not sought the light. We never pay for the mistakes that are done through ignorance. But we do pay for the mistakes we make through sleep. If we make the same mistake twice it is because we have gone to sleep. The lazy man loses both this world and the next.

Ignorance kills innocence. Evil kills innocence. Vanity kills innocence. Hypocrisy is lying to oneself. There is always hope of salvation – when we recognize the truth about ourselves. But the difficult thing is to forgive ourselves. When we admit a mistake openly we do not do it again. We must face everything in ourselves. We know we have negativeness. God has allowed temptations in order to see how strong we are. If we do not make excuses, but face temptations without allowing them to come inside us, they come less and less often.

We stand our ladder of progress on experience. We fall again and again, but our mistakes push us up. We would make more mistakes if we had no experience. Unless we are very much awake we cannot profit by someone else's experience.

Nobody was ever killed by problems. If we could not deal with everything that comes to us, God would not allow it to come. It is not problems but self-pity and worry that kill people. Worry kills people because they allow it. They like to worry. There are no problems that are not imaginary, that are not in the mind. There are stages in our lives; sometimes we are not prepared for them. If we are awake there are no problems. There are many factors in the situations we think are problems, for example, our laziness. It is lack of understanding that makes difficulties. If they are under control they do not take us by surprise. We have to call them problems to give them a name to excuse our ignorance. Human beings love to make problems for themselves because they think it brave to have them. They do not understand that it is stupid – a waste of time.

We do not bear tribulations well because we do not know the right way of seeking spiritual consolations. For this reason he who faithfully works on himself, in himself and for himself more easily endures adversity. Prosperity causes us to fall more often and lower than tribulations. He whose gift costs him nothing will receive nothing of value in return.

All the tribulations we have to go through are very important, for they make us grow. We have to take everything that comes to us as an instrument to grow. We think we ought not to doubt. On the contrary, we *must* doubt. We must never accept anything till we really believe it because we have found out for ourselves why it is true. But we must understand what doubt means. We call many things doubts that are prejudices. We say: 'I doubt that statement' when we are not doubting at all, when it just means that we have already made up our minds that it is not true. On the other hand we should not accept something we are told because we want to accept it, because it would suit us personally if it were true. If we have doubts we should find out, prove to ourselves, whether we are right or not. P. D. Ouspensky always said: 'Don't believe what I say; find out for yourselves.' Often what we think is a doubt is only vanity. We say: 'I wonder whether that is true?' Instead, we should say: 'This is something I don't know. Why don't I believe it? Because I don't understand it.' Then we could study and learn. We should face our lack of understanding and define it.

We have to understand the difference between prejudice and knowledge. Finding four basic reasons for an opinion makes it clear whether it is prejudice or not. Refusing to accept something because it goes against our own type, taste or knowledge is not prejudice.

Prejudice is insincerity. If we really analyse a prejudice we will find that it is not truthful. We must analyse each prejudice for ourselves. We have to recognize why something is a prejudice for us. 'If I believe this, everyone else must believe it' is a prejudice.

Prejudice is limitation. We must not be prejudiced because prejudice means closing ourselves. It is more of a crime to act from prejudice than to kill without knowing. We can work as hard as we like, but if we have prejudice we will never have grace. To receive grace we must be open. 'If you do not believe that I AM, you will die in your sins' – our ways of thinking, which cause our lack of being.

People think it is human to react with prejudice; it is not human, it is animal. To be human means to be open; it means to combine feeling with thinking, to feel other people's reactions and needs. It means being open to high influences and at the same time catching the lowest, heaviest vibrations and putting them together so that light may come. Like electricity, there has to be a positive and a negative pole for a spark to arc between the two. That is what it means to be human – to be real, open, alive to what other people are feeling; to be sensitive to them and at the same time know what is truth, know how to tell them what they need.

We will never be ourselves while we have pre-judice, while we try to judge. We are all mirrors for each other. We see others in reverse to the way we see ourselves. That is why we cannot judge. We must always measure, never judge. What is the difference between measuring and judging? To measure is to observe, to judge is to say why things are and how they ought to be. If I see a fat man and say: 'He looks as though he weighed 200 lbs', I am attempting to measure. If I say: 'That man ought not to be so fat; evidently he eats too much through being greedy', I am trying to judge. How do I know why he is fat? He may be suffering from a glandular disturbance.

We must measure by our own highest standards. We can measure nothing that is inside ourselves. Unless something comes from outside we cannot measure. How to measure? To see, compare. It is truthful to notice that someone is going through a certain phase and why. Trying to find out why is measuring. But to say that the person is an idiot is judging. We cannot judge. In order to judge we would have to know every thing about a person, his complete heredity and all his environment and the influences that had affected him since conception. We would have to have all this knowledge present in our mind simultaneously in order to be able to compare his action with his possibilities. Even God does not judge people while they are still in this world.

Something may be said that appears to us to be unkind, but we do not know the intention with which it was said, nor the effect on the person to whom it was said. If we said it, for us it might be negative, or the person to whom we said it might take it negatively. But we cannot judge whether it was negative between other people. We see that someone is worried and cannot understand how he could be worried by something that would not worry us. We cannot judge. All we can do is to help him turn it to find strength, to turn the situation that is worrying him so that he sees the way out. We cannot judge and we cannot be judged. We can only respect all people, clean ourselves and let true feelings come.

If we were wise we would not judge ourselves. We can judge nothing, because we are not complete. Only a complete being can judge. But we can measure. By measuring we can make comparisons, we can recognize, make contrasts, recognize polarity. By what standard can we measure? Not by anything solid. We have to measure spiritually. We must measure by real feelings, by what is in ourselves. We must just see ourselves as instruments of God to help others. If we talk to others we will see how much or little both we and they know. We must always learn, acquire knowledge.

To be awake enough to give attention to the person we are talking to, this is the work. So often we notice only our own reactions; this is sleep. To be awake means to be aware of ourselves in others. We only notice in others what we have in ourselves. For example, if I see that someone else is lazy it is because I myself am lazy. If I were not lazy I would not see the laziness in the other person. I might see that he was slow and think that he was tired, or find some other reason for his failure to do things properly, but I would not see that he was lazy.

We should feel that there is no badness in others, only in ourselves; that they do wrong through ignorance or blindness. We can never accuse anyone else of being bad for we can never know the real reason why they do what appears to us as wrong. But each person knows for himself that when he does something wrong he could have avoided it. We can never judge others, but our own conscience can judge, not ourselves but

77

our action in a particular case. If we measure and do not judge, others cannot judge us.

Love is everything; it is understanding. We do not love other people for their virtues; how can we tell if a person does something right for vanity? We cannot judge, so we cannot know. We love people for their failings. We love one person because he is vain and needs taking down, another because he is weak and needs confidence. We love people for their needs. We must find the qualities of others and cover their defects with our sins. In this way we can learn not to judge.

VIII

Two men were going home when they met the Master without recognizing Him. He accompanied them on the road and taught them. When they arrived at Emmaus He entered their house and revealed Himself as the Divine Master. Those of us who go by the Fourth Way meet the Master without recognizing Him, and He teaches us. If we invite Him into our house He will manifest Himself to us. For this to happen it is necessary that we should be at home, that is, be present in ourselves.

Truth is to be oneself; when we are full of imagination and of judgment we are not yet ourselves. Everyone has a shallow side and a deep side. People can live from the surface or they can live from inside, from their true inner selves. For this reason each one of us must find his aim. Each individual must find his own aim. It will not be the same for everyone. It may change tomorrow, but it has always to be his own. To find truth we must first know our aim. To know our aim we must first know what we want – sincerely and simply know what we want. Without that, nothing is possible. It is not enough to know it one day and forget it the next. We must be able to express our aim in words, to fix it, to be sure of it. If our aim is vague it is not sure. If it is sure, we can always express it. Real words do not change; do the words of the Lord's Prayer change? Does the word we call our children, the word 'darling', change? We must be solid, we must know our aim and be able to formulate it.

We must always have questions about everything. As soon as we have no questions we stagnate. We must always have questions; whenever we have a question we have an answer.

New circumstances and knowledge are developing at such a speed we have to be very alert to catch them. We can have ideas, but we cannot develop without school to help us digest what we already know, to be able to understand what is the Fourth Way. We cannot find it till we really self-remember. That is harmony. Without school, harmony is impossible. Somebody has to explain it. The proof that the school of harmony is true is that it can be found everywhere. We can find it in books, in conversations, in films, everywhere. If we were clear about our aim we would understand harmony. We would remember ourselves.

Self-remembering does not start within ourselves, but outside ourselves. Everything that starts within ourselves starts with selfishness. If I remember myself before I remember you, that is self-centredness. In self-remembering we bring what is outside inside, in order to collect. We cannot collect what is already in us.

If we were wise we would reflect that which comes from outside us. But not being wise, we cannot work on reflection because we do not know what to reflect. If we work always for our neighbour we will become wise and then we will know what is necessary to reflect. The Fourth Way is understanding, every moment and every situation. An understanding heart is self-remembering. Real self-remembering is not the realization: 'I am here in these clothes, that man is over there in that coat.' Real self-remembering is to put all one's awareness into the needs of others. If, when we speak to someone, although our body remains where it is, our consciousness is with the other person, that is self-remembering. If we concentrate on ourselves we cannot be aware of other people. But if we are aware of other people that means that we are aware of ourselves. It is easy to understand. If we try to look at our bodies we can see only part of them, and never our faces. But if we use a mirror we can see more of our bodies and our faces as well. If we use a combination of mirrors we can even see our own backs. In the same way, if we try to observe ourselves direct, we can see almost nothing, but if we observe someone else we can see more of ourselves reflected in him, and if we observe many people, really notice them, we will probably get a very good picture of ourselves indeed. We can have many illusions about ourselves and our motives, but if we see other people's reactions to us, our illusions will disappear and gradually we will see ourselves as we really are. And when that happens we will see that other people are just like ourselves and that we are just like other people – in fact, that we are all alike. Then we will no longer have the feeling of 'I', of separateness, either the proud feeling or the miserable feeling, both of which are only vanity.

To understand why self-remembering is not called 'remembering others' or 'remembering God' we must understand the idea of the mirror. People think that the words 'Thou shalt love the Lord with all thy heart ... and thy neighbour as thyself' should read 'and thy neighbour and thyself', taking the last part to refer to self-respect. That too; but if we remember the idea of the mirror we will understand the original reading.

We must learn to harmonize body with spirit. We must remember our physical body, our soul and our spirit; remember ourselves. We cannot remember ourselves till we forget ourselves. If we are aware of our surroundings and of our eyes seeing them we are not thinking of ourselves. Our eyes that we see with are not ourselves. There is a tremendous difference between thinking about ourselves and remembering ourselves. We have not forgotten our name and address although we are not thinking about them all the time. The spirit always knows and remembers it is in the presence of God. Not only the spirit; the body does too. Although it takes it for granted, it does not forget.

Spirit is pure – the purest thing we have. We must purify our instincts. Little by little we have to take out what is impure in us in order to make room for the pure distillation from the spirit. We do it by self-remembering – that is, by being alert and open, using the whole of us, instinct, heart and intellect.

There is hypocrisy in all of us. We all have an enemy in ourselves. But we also have an angel on the other side. There is one person who will never fail us, our Guardian Angel, if we make the habit of asking him for help. We must choose which side we want to go, which way we want to lean. If we choose right we choose by self-remembering. It is a very wise work, but we must understand it right.

Each person has to create self-remembering for himself in his own way, even in his own religion. It does not matter what religion we have; Allah and God is the same person. The only Master is God, the only teacher is ourself. Nobody can force others to believe him. Everybody has to find his own way, his own understanding, his own alert conscience. We have to accept by ourselves, for ourselves, what self-remembering means for us. Self-remembering is the well of virtues, the food of the soul. Remembrance is everything. Self-remembering is divinity.

It is very important to know what is self-remembering, what is soul, what is conscience. Every individual should find out what it is for him, by developing his mind to accept, to recognize. Only by self-remembering can we dominate every circumstance necessary for the whole perfection of living. We can do it if we want it and aim for it. We must not jump to conclusions, but study thoroughly.

Understanding takes away fear. The first step in self-remembering is self-assurance. If we have self-assurance we do not mind the opinion of others.

We must connect earth and sky, live between earth and sky. When we pray, when we help others, then we connect earth and sky. There is so much beauty in the world; when we look at all that beauty and perfection, how can we help self-remembering? When we self-remember we remember God. To recognize beauty is self-remembering; to communicate with the high, that is self-remembering; to feel beauty, to feel truth, that is self-remembering. Self-remembering is not imagination. People think they are self-remembering when they control their feelings. That is not self-remembering. Self-remembering is awareness of the presence of God.

We do not understand the big work of God. We cannot explain what white is or pure is; we have to *be* it and show it. When someone has really learned to do things for God and not for himself, he really acts for love of God and the devil cannot touch him. The devil is not interested in people he is sure of, in the people who can be counted on to do wrong. It is the people who are really striving to love God that the devil is interested in. There is a personal devil, but he is in us.

God is not in everything. He is only in clean things. How can we think He is in men when they are cruel? He sees it, yes; he sees everything, but is not in everything.

Fear of God is recognition of our own level. First must be fear of God. When there is fear there is purity. When there is purity, non-attachment to this world, there is charity. Fear of God does not come from Him but from ourselves, when we know that we are not clean. When repentence follows the fear of God, then we are clean and love Him without fear. Our whole being changes if we even think about repentence and try to understand what it means. Only people who are clean feel love of God; then there is no fear. 'Perfect love casteth out fear.'

God is justice and mercy. When we are judged it will be word by word, act by act and thought by thought, and we shall be paid with love. Otherwise we could never be forgiven and received into heaven.

Christ threw the money-changers out of the temple because they were bargaining with God. Only God knows whether we are trying to bargain with Him. Often people go to church to bargain with God; sooner or later they get thrown out, in one form or another.

All the saints had strong tempers. By struggling with their tempers and turning them positive they became saints. Unless there is a temper to be turned positive, used positively, there is no strength of character. It needs tremendous strength of character to become a saint.

Superstition is an insult to God because it denies our understanding that we are taken care of. If we want to go forward we must look forward with faith; nothing wrong can happen to us. If we are really serving God our day-to-day needs will be provided for. If we want luxuries, that is different, but our needs will be looked after. If we give ourselves to this work our real needs will be looked after – if we have no vanities.

Generosity is the sister of charity. Charity is the transposition of love to the level of the spirit. Only a man who reaches that will be transported to the Kingdom of Heaven. Charity is quality, not quantity; it is intention, not extension.

Faith is love of God; hope is love of ourselves; charity is love of our neighbour. The more will, the more charity; the more charity, the more love. Faith is the acceptance of a reality which we feel but do not understand. Hope is confidence in the love of God. He has hope who has confidence, he who has confidence has love, he has love who gives his attention to others.

Love is not voluntary; it is a grace. He who has received the grace to pray has received no small mercy from God. We should pray for the grace to love God. There is no love that is not a grace – love of flowers, love of animals, love of people – all love is a grace. The greater the soul the more God's love can be transformed. Soul is will; it takes will to transform the love of God into charity.

When we are in love there is no sacrifice we would not make for the other person. Why do we not do the same for God? We are constantly thanking people for the things they give us, but how often do we think of thanking Our Lord?

Dark moments only come when we have no faith. Dark moments only come when we shut the door on God. We must open the door and say: 'The Lord is there; blessed be the Lord.' To close the door and say: 'Lord, take away the darkness!' is an offence to God. The sun shines and He made it; all the world testifies to the presence of God. He says to us: 'You have will; open your eyes and look at Me.' We do not need to say: 'I will seek God', when all the time God is seeking us.

If I know that one day I shall see God, if I think of that, how can I help smiling with happiness? If I am shown day and night all the beautiful things there are in the world, surely I should smile. If I see children coming, and they are the true thing, life that is coming, the future, for that I ought to smile.

To laugh is not real, to cry is not real, but to smile is real. We should go through the work smiling. We are filled with the love of God when we feel happy. Happiness is the realization of the union of everything clean with God. Prayer makes us real, really clean. When we pray we are revealing our real selves, without hiding anything.

How should we pray? By real feelings. We must sincerely feel what we want. We must learn to harmonize our thoughts with our feelings and connect our feelings with the high. One of the ways we learn truth is by emphasizing our connection with a higher level.

Thought is effective when it directs the irradiations caused by our feelings. Prayer is good thought intensified by being sent to God. A good thought sent direct to someone helps him in proportion to the strength of the irradiations of our love for him; the same thought sent to God is intensified much as the rays of the sun are intensified by a burning-glass. Prayers are our highest irradiations magnified by God. That is why prayer is so powerful.

How should we pray? When we give our hearts to God then it does not matter what words we use; we are really praying. When we offer God our hearts with real attention to the intention, so that there is no wanting for ourselves and no not-wanting for ourselves when all we do is God's doing through us, then we are really alive. Then we see God; He ceases to be an idea that we think about, but a reality that we can see. Then we see Him and feel Him, for He is in our own heart. Our heart is a mirror in which we see the reflection of the world; if God is in our heart, we see Him everywhere.

Even if we do not know how to pray and we say: 'Help me, God!' we already have His help. Prayer does not have to be in words; there is prayer of the body and of the heart as well as of the mind. There was a man whose heart and mind were dry; he went into his garden and knocked two stones together, saying: 'I can find no other way to pray.' Do you not think God heard him?

Christ is so great, so high; sometimes we wonder how our prayers can reach Him. When anyone says the Lord's Prayer even the archangels withdraw so that the son may speak directly with his Father without anyone else overhearing.

Sometimes when we pray we feel something. Then next day by imagination we want to feel the same thing and so stop the new thing that we *could* feel. Praying is directing the heart to God. When we really pray we do not go into words, we go into God. We pray when we do not think of ourselves, but instead give ourselves wholly into the hands of God. The path to God has been open since the beginning of the world.

The Holy Spirit appeared as a tongue of flame over the head of each apostle. He hovers like a flame over each one of us. When we are negative we disconnect ourselves from Him; when we are positive we reach up and connect ourselves with the flame and its light shines through us.

Faith is connection with God, inspiration, grace. Grace comes from above. Christ came by grace. It was a grace that He came. He came from a virgin by grace. He came in a body by grace. We love by grace. By grace we can do anything. We have to keep ourselves in grace and keep our connection with Christ. By keeping our grace we leave all the heaviness of this world and keep the lightness of above. And how do we do this? By prayer.

To invoke the name of God is to pray. To invoke the name of God directly from the heart is to put ourselves directly in contact with God. May it be soon that we live with the name of God always in our hearts.